T0102920

Be Selfish! Give More!

Keira Cecily

BALBOA.PRESS
A DIVISION OF HAY HOUSE

Balboa Press books may be ordered through booksellers or by contacting:

Balboa Press
A Division of Hay House
1663 Liberty Drive
Bloomington, IN 47403
www.balboapress.com
844-682-1282

Because of the dynamic nature of the Internet, any web addresses or
links contained in this book may have changed since publication and may
no longer be valid. The views expressed in this work are solely those
of the author and do not necessarily reflect the views of the publisher,
and the publisher hereby disclaims any responsibility for them.

The author of this book does not dispense medical advice or prescribe
the use of any technique as a form of treatment for physical, emotional,
or medical problems without the advice of a physician, either directly
or indirectly. The intent of the author is only to offer information
of a general nature to help you in your quest for emotional and
spiritual well-being. In the event you use any of the information in
this book for yourself, which is your constitutional right, the author
and the publisher assume no responsibility for your actions.

Any people depicted in stock imagery provided by Getty Images are
models, and such images are being used for illustrative purposes only.
Certain stock imagery © Getty Images.

Print information available on the last page.

ISBN: 979-8-7652-2834-0 (sc)
ISBN: 979-8-7652-2835-7 (e)

Balboa Press rev. date: 06/02/2022

Greetings!

My name is Keira. Thank you for embarking on this Journey of Self Care. Care of your Mind, your Body, and your Energy.

The main goal of this book is to help you realize a very important but often ignored fact... Taking care of yourself is essential to your ability to be helpful to the ones you love.

Loving you comes first. Being selfish with your time, your thoughts, and your emotions, is how you can be the most effective and efficient in your daily interactions.

It is how you can Give More! You may need to break some habits...bad habits and develop new ones. Ones that allow you to make yourself THE priority.

It isn't difficult, but there are those who would have you believe it's impossible and selfish...Be Selfish! My hope is that by the end of this journey, you will find strength that you may have lost, power you may have denied and instincts that you learn to trust. Throughout the book there are various Note Pages to jot down your thoughts and ideas on how to Be Selfish! to Give More! Apply those thoughts, meditate on those ideas, and discover, re-discover, transform, and mostly have fun with this fresh take on just being you.

KEIRA CECILY

Set Boundaries

SETTING
BOUNDARIES
IS AN ACT OF
RESPECT AND
LOVE
TOWARDS
YOURSELF

What does it mean to set boundaries?
Boundaries can be defined as the limits we set with other
people, which indicate what is acceptable and unacceptable
in their behaviour towards us.
In doing this, you may feel like you are losing people. . .
and truthfully you are. You lose those abusive,
manipulating, control freaks who could very well destroy
your mental health and peace of mind.
Let them go!
What you won't lose are Real friends,
Real opportunities, and Real relationships
All that stays right where it is.
Ready to welcome you.
Ready to support you.
Ready to keep you growing.
Setting boundaries is how you love yourself first, even if
it means disappointing others. This act of self preservation
enables you to give more of yourself purposely and
effectively.

Set Bounderies

What bounderies can I set today?

Stop Allowing

Stop asking why they keep Doing it and start asking why you keep Allowing it

People will do only as much as you allow them to.
They will only expect what you have allowed them to expect from you.

If it is a fear of disappointing others that holds you back from setting limitations, start with limits that only you must honor. It is a great way to practice. For example ... to stop allowing outside influences on how your day flows, no email, or social media before meditating.

Another example... to stop allowing the misuse of your time and/or the time of another person, show up ten minutes early for every appointment and/or meeting.

These are a couple that I have personally used, however, I have many more that I have held as standard in various relationships, both business and personal. Very often we feel setting limits are harsh or mean, but they are intentional acts of kindness to your number one person... YOU. You are giving yourself permission to take care of YOU. When you honor your personal parameters, you are saying ...

I AM Important to me and to my loved ones, so taking care of myself matters.

Stop Allowing

What can I stop allowing today?

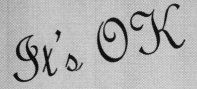

It's OK

IT'S OK TO CHANGE YOUR MIND.

IT'S OK TO GO IN A DIFFERENT DIRECTION
THAN OTHERS EXPECT FROM YOU.

IT'S OKAY TO SAY THIS NO LONGER WORKS
FOR ME.

It is OK to cancel a commitment, don't do it if you're
not feeling it.
It is OK to not answer a call, no answer is an answer
that may be needed.
It is OK to change your mind, sometimes forward
thought kicks in after you said yes.
It is OK to want to be alone, every emotion doesn't need
another's opinion.
It is OK to take a day off,
sometimes it takes a whole day to recharge, regain and
reset.
It is OK to do Nothing, if you don't choose to have a
seat, your body will choose for you.
It is OK to say no, No!
Understood in every language and is the best way to
protect your body,
your mind, and your energy.

It is OK

	Whatever I need to change today is OK!
●	
●	

Break Patterns

May you have the courage to break
the patterns in your life that are no
longer serving you.

Examine All Patterns!

Friendship Patterns.

Work Patterns.

Mindset Patterns.

Gratitude Patterns.

Money Patterns.

Health Patterns.

Patterns are things that have occurred way too many times to be a coincidence. A pattern will keep recurring until the lesson you need to get from it is learned. Once that happens, you are usually able to break free, and even better, evolve to a new pattern with a more positive outcome. In fact, this new pattern will Always result in your favor. Remember, patterns aren't necessarily a bad thing, however you must be sure it continues to work for you. For your growth. For your success. For your Peace. That moment when you can finally say a bad pattern has been broken, is the most gratifying feeling.

Oh, and when you recognize that pattern that has worked all along and continue to work for your good...

Be Thankful.

Break Patterns

What patterns can I break or change today?

Just Breathe

With each Breathe
I am bringing

calm and peace

to my
mind, body, and soul.

Are you breathing correctly?

Breathing is something most do robotically.

However, breathes should be taken intentionally.

What that means is using your breath to increase

awareness, mindfulness, and peace.

Ready to harness the power of your Inhales and

Exhales? Let's Begin....

start by sitting or lying down in a comfortable position.

Your eyes can be open or closed.

Now, Inhale for 4 counts, and Exhale for 4-6 counts.

The exhale should be just a little longer.

Inhale Confidence - Exhale Doubt

Inhale Faith - Exhale Worry

Inhale Calm - Exhale Chaos

Inhale Wellness- Exhale Illness

Inhale Peace - Exhale Disruption

Inhale Gratitude - Exhale Entitlement

Say the words aloud and repeat until you feel stress

and frustration is washing away. Once you learn the art

of Inhaling and Exhaling, you will most certainly feel

better, and you may even notice that you've developed a

little extra resilience.

Just Breathe

Remember: Inhale for 4 counts, and Exhale for 5-6 counts
Use this page to note your Inhales and Exhales

Celebrate Accomplishments

Celebrating your accomplishments
can boost your confidence,
help to stave off burnout,
and fuel our continued success.

A Win is A Win! Big or Small.

Most of us have several things we are seeking to
accomplish at one time.

Some write them down. Some just go for it spontaneously.

Some make a well thought out plan.

No matter what the method is, there is a chance it will
work and an equal chance that it won't.

But when it does...Celebrate!

We should all be proud of ourselves when we can check
something...anything... off the list.

You completed a workout ✓

You cleaned your office ✓

You tried something new ✓

You started a business ✓

You took some classes ✓

You got a promotion ✓

You handled a difficult client ✓

You bought a new house ✓

You did it! You are Here! You are Moving, Growing
and Elevating! Don't Stop Now!

Celebrate Accomplishments

Make a list and check things off as you go!
Watch how you feel.

No Worries

Worry does not rid tomorrow of its sorrow. It rids today of its strength.

Very often we tend to put an enormous amount of energy into worrying.

Will this plan work? Will this person help? Should I leave? Should I stay? Know & Believe without a doubt that there are no mistakes and even if it appears as one, you should come out of it with a lesson; therefore, it is not. How do you know if that person, situation, or physical placement is for you? If it educates you, elevates you, motivates you and quite simply comes to you easily, chances are it was Meant to Be! Keep your vibration high and in tune with your Source and everything you touch or that touches you will Always be for your Benefit...meant specifically for YOU. Take some time today to reflect on the troubles of your heart and the worries on your Soul. Then I want you to Let them go! Each person has a specific purpose; however, we are all here to Learn and Grow. That cannot happen if you are being weighed down by worry and fear. Search your soul and the desires of your heart and if there is anything there not taking you to the next level, preventing you from changing your mindset or not elevating your vibration ...

Let. It. Go!!

No Worries

What can I let go of today?

The Commitment

Commitment means staying loyal to what you said you were going to do long after the mood you said it in has left you.

Making a commitment involves dedicating yourself to something, like a person or a cause.

A commitment obligates you to do something. Well, Commit to Committing to You! What does that mean? Check in with yourself.

Talk to yourself!

• • • • • • • • • • • •

Yes, even scold yourself when you know you are not on task.

Eat right!

• • • • • • • •

Read labels and be purposeful regarding what you put in your body.

Exercise!

• • • • • • • •

10-minute cardio, 5 push-ups, 10 squats... a little something is better than nothing at all.

Meditate!

• • • • • • • •

Get your spirit, mind, and body in Agreement that your most important task, your most diligent actions, your most consistent effort... is You Elevating You!

Commit to You!

	How can I commit to myself today?
●	
●	

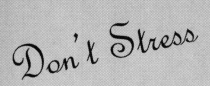

Stop Stressing. Take a
deep breath.
Everything will be okay.

Whew!! The past 2 years have been very stressful for many.

Much more for some than others.

We will not handle our stress the same, however, we should all be proud of ourselves.

When you wanted to cry, you laughed instead. When you wanted to beat yourself up about how much weight you gained, you worked out instead. You tried new things.

You took some classes.

You started a business. You showed up for the Zoom calls, and not just the work ones...the Birthdays, the Baby Showers, the Weddings, and Maybe even the Funerals. (May Everyone we have lost Rest in Paradise)

All the virtual events you could have opted out of, yet you were There! You smiled, you sang, and you enjoyed yourself.

Keep that Stress Free Energy today, tomorrow, next week and next month!

You Got This!

Stress Free Zone

List some things causing you to stress
then write an action to reverse the energy

●

●

Stay Focused

STARVE YOUR DISTRACTIONS. FEED YOUR FOCUS.

Fact!!!

That which you focus on, will manifest in your reality!

Be Intentional!

Keep Your Focus!

I am focused on Purpose

I am focused on Wellness

I am focused on Branding

I am focused on Improving

I am focused on Achieving goals

I am focused on being a Blessing

I am focused on Good Energy

What's your focus??

Stay Focused

Write down the things you want to focus on and create a manifesting affirmation for each one.

I Want to Discover More?

Book a live session with me at

Simplymeet.me/touchedbykeiracecily

services offered:

Life Coach Session

Meditation Session

Career Coach

Book me as your Doula

Book me for your Wedding

Touchedby KeiraCecily.com
(lauching September 2022)